NEW YORK'S RANGERS
The Icemen Cometh

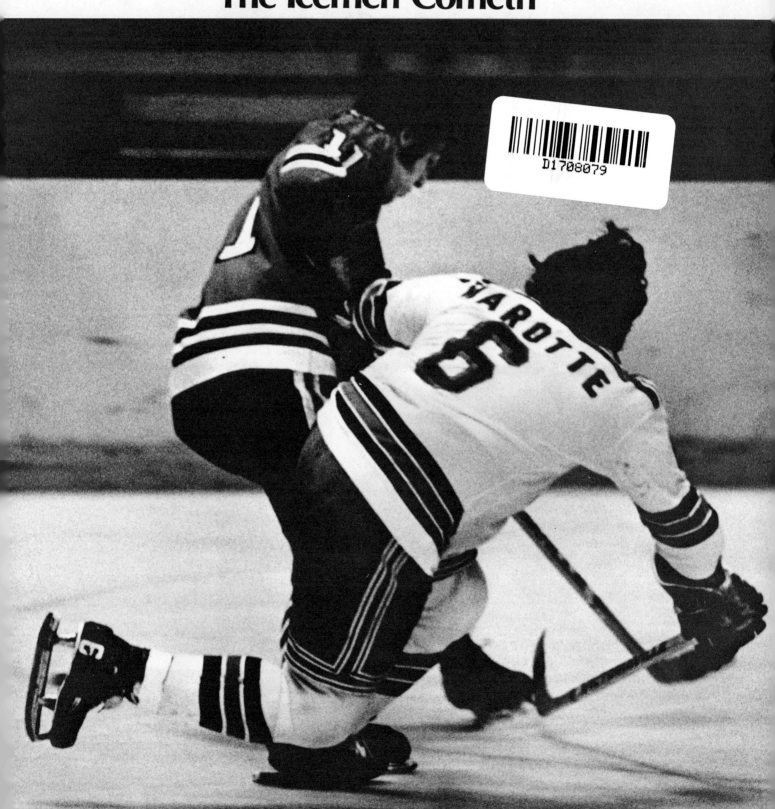

NEW YORK'S RANGERS
The Icemen Cometh

by Stan Fischler

Photography/Melchior Di Giacomo

Introduction by Marv Albert

A Stuart L. Daniels Book

PRENTICE-HALL, INC.
Englewood Cliffs, New Jersey

Art Directors: Suzanne Esper
            Renate Lude
Editorial Associate: Andrew H. Kulak
Special Projects Director: Elizabeth J. Cossa

Published by Prentice-Hall, Inc.
Englewood Cliffs, New Jersey

Printed in the United States of America T
Prentice-Hall International, Inc., London
Prentice-Hall of Australia, Pty. Ltd., Sydney
Prentice-Hall of Canada, Ltd., Toronto
Prentice-Hall of India Private Ltd., New Delhi
Prentice-Hall of Japan, Inc., Tokyo

Library of Congress Catalog Card Number: 74-9237

ISBN: 0-13-620567-4

PHOTOGRAPHERS' NOTE

I would like to thank the following Cyclops Team photographers who share with me the credit for assembling the photographs in this book: Peter Mecca, Jack Mecca and Michael Albanese.

Mel DiGiacomo

DEDICATION

To Dick Kaplan and Lew Gillenson who helped get me started in this business.

Stan Fischler

ACKNOWLEDGMENTS

The author wishes to thank Richard Friedman, Howard Hyman, Peter Ginsberg, Nancy Demmon, Melinda Muniz, Barry Wilner and Larry Zeidel who helped so much in the preparation of this book.

"wait 'til next year"
by marv albert

Sportscaster Marv Albert, the voice of the New York Rangers.

Having grown up in the shadows of Brooklyn's now-departed Ebbets Field, and having rooted passionately for the old Dodgers, I learned the virtues of patience and fortitude when it comes to backing the home team.

It was the Dodgers who coined the expression, "Wait 'til next year. They made it a part of our sports language. Decades passed—pennants came and went—before Brooklyn finally won a World Series.

Now, hopefully, it's the Rangers' turn to bring home a world championship, hockey's Stanley Cup. For nearly a decade I've been saying, "Wait 'til next year," hoping that, for the Blueshirts, next year really is *this* year.

Unfortunately, the Rangers, good as they have been, to date have yet to put it all together.

But now I'm convinced that Emile Francis has put together the proper ingredients for an NHL title. The acquisition of dynamic Derek Sanderson and the infusion of new young blood will give Gotham hockey fans the kind of pizzazz they're looking for.

As they say, "patience is a virtue," and nobody has been more virtuous than the Ranger fans.

For their sake, I hope the Blueshirts come through. I believe they will, just as the Dodgers once did when Johnny Podres pitched them to glory and the grail.

SO, GO, RANGERS, GO!

Defenseman Jim Neilson (15) shields the Ranger goal while the Ranger goalie is out of position.

the elusive silver cup

The annual tragedy that befalls the New York Rangers in their playoff quest for the Stanley Cup has been mystifying Madison Square Garden fans ever since 1940. That's the last time a Ranger unit claimed possession of Lord Stanley's silver trophy. Since then, no other National Hockey League club has been so singularly frustrated in its pursuit of that big prize.

While the Chicago Black Hawks, the Blueshirt's closest rival in post-season failure, have a full-fledged curse (the Muldoon jinx) to contend with, the New Yorkers can find no real explanation—superstitious or otherwise, to console them. In the Black Hawks' early days coach Pete Muldoon, fired by owner Major Frederic McLaughlin put a "hoodoo" on the club.

Some solace can be taken in the realization that the Blueshirts do have it in them to take the whole ball of wax—they have certainly shown that potential on many occasions.

9

early success

Lester Patrick, known as the Silver Fox, managed the New York Rangers from 1926 to 1946. His coaching career with the Blueshirts ran from 1926 thru the 1938–39 season.

The New York Rangers were spawned in 1926 when fight promoter Tex Rickard became fascinated with the game of ice hockey and decided that a team could be enthusiastically supported in New York City. He retained young Conn Smythe, then a successful hockey manager in Toronto, to organize a winning sextet for New York. It was assumed that the team would be called "Tex's Rangers" after its founder. That was shortened to the Rangers, and the name remains.

After getting the puck rolling, Smythe decided he couldn't contend with Madison Square Garden's front-office hassles and he soon resigned his post. His replacement was Lester "Silver Fox" Patrick, a promoter who had come to New York from the defunct Pacific Coast Hockey Association.

Center Jean Ratelle has been a productive goal scorer with the Rangers and leads the attack for the famous Goal-A-Game line.

From the very start Patrick collected the nucleus of a potential hockey dynasty. Lorne Chabot was his goaltender, and there were other greats such as center Frank Boucher, the Cook Brothers—Bun and Bill, and defensemen Ching Johnson and Taffy Abel.

So powerful were the 1926-27 Rangers, that they brashly overtook established NHL clubs and finished atop the American Division. The headiness of their accomplishment might have caused a bit of overconfidence in the first year Blueshirts and they were rudely and swiftly eliminated in the first round of the 1927 playoffs.

Entering their second season with a division championship already under their belts, or rather, suspenders, the 1927-28 Rangers had a tough act to follow. Undaunted, they went about their task in workmanlike fashion and gave every indication of being a powerful factor in the league for seasons to come.

Finishing second to the Boston Bruins in the American Division, the Rangers defeated the Pittsburgh Pirates in the opening round of the playoffs. Next came the Bruins in the semifinals, and the Rangers breezed by, capturing the two-game, total goals series.

Now the New Yorkers faced the powerful Montreal Maroons in the finals of the Stanley Cup playoffs. (Montreal boasted two NHL teams in those days, as did New York.) The series was a three-of-five games affair, and the Maroons had an almost insurmountable psychological edge.

Ringling Brothers, Barnum & Bailey circus had priority over hockey games at Madison Square Garden in those days, and the Rangers were barred from the friendly home arena. After attempts to find an alternative "home" site proved fruitless, it was decided to play all five games at the hostile Montreal Forum.

The veteran Maroons skated to a 2–0 win in the first game and the Rangers knew they were involved in a tough series. Just exactly how tough would be known in the very next game.

13

There was no score early in game number two when Maroon center Nels Stewart, one of the most feared shooters of the day, let loose a blast that caught Rangers' goaltender Lorne Chabot squarely in the face. Remember, this was in the days before masks. Dazed and bleeding, Chabot had to leave the nets. One of the most remarkable stories in sports history had begun to unfold.

In those early days, dressing a spare goaltender was unheard of. In fact, very few teams even carried an extra netminder on their roster at all. Chabot's injury was a major catastrophe at the very least. The question remained—who could play goal for the Rangers. The Maroons were gloating, confident that victory was now assured. They refused New York the services of two minor league goaltenders who were in the stands watching the game.

In desperation, coach Patrick stepped forward and said, "Boys, I'm going to play goal. Check as you've never checked before fellows, and protect an old man," the Silver Fox beseeched his players.

Patrick, who was forty-five years old at the time, had had some goaltending experience, but he knew he was acting more with his heart than his head as he donned the bulky pads and skated out to meet the powerful Maroons. Rallying around their ancient leader, the Rangers kept even with the Montrealers until the third period when Bill Cook broke in and put the Rangers ahead, 1–0.

The minutes ticked away and it looked as if the series would be tied at one game apiece until Nels Stewart knotted the contest. Six minutes remained in regulation time and still tied, the game went into overtime. Feeling the shift in momentum, the Maroons pressed relentlessly in the overtime period, only to be blunted time and time again by the Rangers and their improvised netminder. Finally, at 7:05 of overtime, Frank Boucher silenced the Forum throng by pouncing on a loose puck and rifling it past the Montreal goalie to tie the series for the Rangers.

An emotional Blueshirt team carried their trembling leader off the ice after his inspired effort. He had allowed but one goal, Stewart's, and had shown the Rangers that they could do it without a regular goalie and without the home ice advantage.

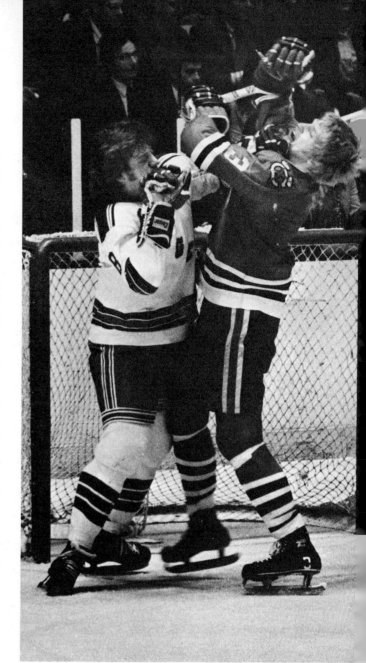

Steve Vickers and Chicago defenseman Keith Magnuson get their sticks up after Vickers penetrated the Black Hawks crease.

Defenseman Jim Neilson, the "Chief," carries the puck out from behind his net, pursued by Frank Mahovlich.

There was not much time for the Rangers to rest on their laurels. The Maroons came right back in the third game, blanking the New York sextet, 2–0. Montreal required only one more win to end the Ranger season and take the cup. The Broadway Blues were not about to roll over and play dead. Frank Boucher scored in the fourth game and his Ranger mates made it stand as the New Yorkers won 1–0 and forced a fifth and deciding contest.

The Maroons were favored in the finale, but on this night, in this playoff, the Rangers were destiny's darlings. Patrick's inspired guidance, the heroics of Frank Boucher, and the acrobatics of an obscure goalie named Joe "Red Light" Miller combined to beat the Maroons in the fifth game and New York had it's first Staney Cup.

The next five seasons were successful for the Broadway icemen in each of which they finished in third place or better and qualified for the playoffs. While their dreams of a Stanley Cup dynasty that had been so deliriously predicted were not realized, they did reach the Cup finals twice in those five seasons, winning the centerpiece again in 1932-33.

The 1932-33 Rangers were still built around the fabled Boucher line and defensive great, Ching Johnson, but time had forced some changes. Lester Patrick had moved into the club presidency and left the goaltending heroics to a chap named Andy Aitkenhead. The club was maturing and wanted to win another shot at the Stanley Cup before confronting middle age.

Having finished in third place, the Rangers' quarterfinal opponents were the tradition-rich Montreal Canadiens. The New Yorkers outgunned the Frenchmen in a two-game, total goals series, and then made quick work of the Detroit Red Wings in the semifinals, six goals to three. Once again, the Rangers were in the best-of-five final series—their opponents, the Toronto Maple Leafs and ex-Rangers' manager, Conn Smythe.

This series was never in doubt, as the Rangers stormed past the Leafs in four games, dropping only the third. The Blueshirt victory was sealed in the fourth game by Bill Cook's sudden death goal. For the second time in their brief history, the Rangers had won the treasured Stanley Cup.

Brad Park, now the Rangers' captain, takes a Bruin out of play.

rebuilding and another cup

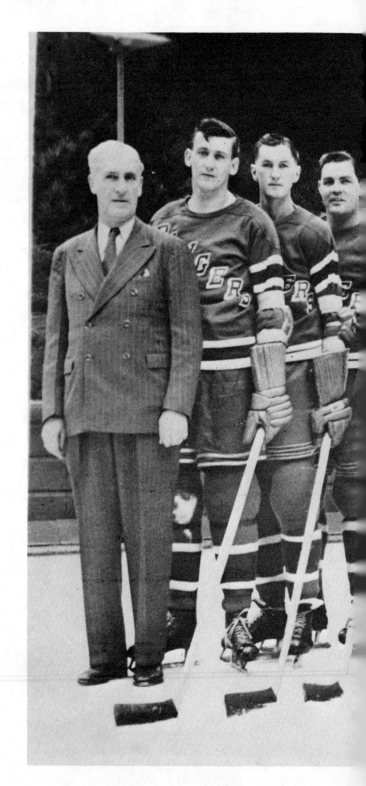

Although the Blueshirts qualified for the playoffs in all but one of the next seven seasons, that period in the late nineteen-thirties was basically one of rebuilding. Boucher, the Cooks, and Johnson were getting old, so Patrick organized a player development farm system that yielded the likes of goalie Dave Kerr, defensemen Art Coulter, Babe Pratt, Ott Heller, and Muzz Patrick (Lester's son), and forwards Neil and Mac Colville and Alex Shibicky.

By the time the 1939-1940 season arrived, Boucher had hung up his skates and replaced Patrick behind the Ranger bench. The Boucher era became a renaissance of modern ice-hockey with Frank introducing such revolutionary developments as the "box defense" for short-handed situations, aggressive penalty killing, and removing the goaltender for a sixth skater "on the fly." All of Boucher's innovations soon became standard operating procedure for modern day hockey.

The 1942–43 New York Rangers were managed by Lester Patrick (at left) and boasted such stars as Phil Watson, and Bryan Hextall. Coach and former Ranger star Frank Boucher is second from right.

Gilles Villemure stays with the action while his defensemen are out of position and braces himself against a Bruin attacker.

Boucher's 1939-1940 Rangers have been called one of the best Broadway teams in history. Finishing second in the NHL's Eastern Division, the New Yorker's semi-final opponents were the first place Boston Bruins. New York outlasted the Beantowners four games to two and then moved on to face the Toronto Maple Leafs in the Cup finals.

With the series tied at two games apiece, the circus invaded Madison Square Garden and again the Rangers were homeless. They were now faced with the unhappy prospect of playing the remaining three games at Maple Leaf Gardens.

New York's star-studded lineup included Phil Watson, Bryan Hextall, Dutch Hiller, the Patricks and the Colvilles. With this cast of characters, the Rangers were not to be denied even if the contests had been held on the frozen waters of the St. Lawrence River. In dramatic fashion, the Rangers took only two more games to dispose of the Leafs and, once again, to take the Stanley Cup; both wins coming in sudden death overtime.

Once again, the hoopla that followed the Rangers' victory rang with predictions of dynasties, powerhouses, and a great big lock on the Stanley Cup. Only one thing went wrong though—something called World War II.

The war years decimated the NHL and the Rangers were riddled with more losses than any other club. Not again did the Blueshirts recapture their winning ways until the mid-1950's and the 1960's. Since those last, glorious, cup-winning moments of 1940, the Rangers have qualified for the playoffs in only sixteen of thirty-four seasons. And, as everyone knows, even though they reached the final round twice and the semifinals an incredible ten times, they have not since won the coveted award.

All this, and still no Cup. But they did do it way back when—ah, those were the days, my friend.

season of conflict

One month after the 1972-73 season was a painful memory, Emile Francis announced his decision to back away from his coaching duties. Larry Popein, a minor league coach, and ex-Rangers' player, was named coach with Emile continuing as general manager. Everyone believed that in the coming season something big would have to happen.

Happen it did. Granted, the 1973-74 season will not be fondly remembered by many Rangers or their fans, it was eventful—memorable in many ways.

Quite naturally, the burning question in the minds of all Rangers' watchers was how would the combination of Popein-plus-New York Rangers meld. Francis had been admired and depended upon by the New Yorkers, perhaps to an extreme. Popein, by contrast, was distant and somewhat aloof. He had said from the very beginning that the system to be used would remain, basically, Emile's. He hinted, however, that the coach was going to crack the whip. Before long the new concoction started smoldering.

Rod Gilbert is noted for his strong skating style, a flair for scoring and popularity with the fans. He played on a line which shattered all team records and became the second highest scoring trio in NHL annals.

Gilles Villemure is a consistent goaltender who makes tough saves look easy.

Rod Gilbert comes in on a breakaway; Minnesota goalie Cesare Maniago is in his sights.

The Rangers got off to a strong start in the first two games of the 1973-74 season, winning handily over the Detroit Red Wings and Pittsburgh Penguins. Optimism was contagious. All three lines were skating well, both Giacomin and Villemure looked sharp in goal. A promising fourth line of youngsters Mike Murphy, Gene Carr, and Tom Williams began to look like a future legacy for the Rangers.

The Los Angeles Kings invaded Madison Square Garden for the third game of the season. The Rangers played well against the much improved west coast sextet and the two teams skated to a well-deserved 1–1 tie. But the score was not the big story that Sunday evening —not by a long shot.

Rod Gilbert, who was closing in on the all-time Ranger scoring mark, was conspicuously absent as veteran Bobby Rousseau manned his normal right wing spot on the GAG line. There had been no report of injury, yet Gilbert was not suited up for the game.

"It was my reason," Popein tersely non-explained, after the game, adding, "It's a routine thing."

Is it routine to bench one of the league's top right wingers? The story began to unfold. It seems that the new Ranger coach had called an 11 A.M. team meeting at Madison Square Garden. This seemed to create a problem. When Emile Francis was coach, his team meetings were always called for high noon and old habits do die hard. So when Rod Gilbert walked into the meeting room at 11:30 A.M., all he found were empty seats and a fuming Popein.

Gilbert, obviously not wanting to rock the ship more than necessary, accepted his punishment, but felt he had been slighted.

"I think he (Popein) made a mistake," said Gilbert.

Striking a blow for employee solidarity, the Rangers team stood with Gilbert.

Why embarrass a guy like Rod that way?" implored a teammate. "Why make Rod the scapegoat?"

Gilbert did his best to make little of the matter. "As far as I'm concerned, it's over." In reality, it was far from over. What the Rangers would later call a "lack of communication" between Popein and the team was beginning to emerge.

Ed Giacomin is about to make a save on
a rising shot.

Bobby Rousseau, a swift skating, quick shooting right wing, starred for many years with the Montreal Canadiens. He came to New York in 1971 from the Minnesota North Stars.

"It's a very touchy thing that could cause problems," warned Brad Park. "Rod's one guy who doesn't miss practices."

With Gilbert reinstated, and apologies everywhere, the Rangers blanked a weak St. Louis Blues team 4–0. Then, more problems. The next seven Rangers outings produced one measly tie, and six losses. Slowly, the atmosphere in the Ranger dressing room began to fill with apprehension. Would there be a shake-up? Who would go first?

"If we don't get off to a good start, you can be sure that Francis will start moving bodies in all directions," observed an unnamed Rangers veteran. "And," he added, "if we don't win the Cup this year, we'll all be gone."

The Rangers' horrendous slump dragged on. They dropped a game to the lowly Islanders, as well as crumbling before the Canadiens, Black Hawks, Penguins, Maple Leafs, and Kings. The one game that they managed to tie was against the punchless Vancouver Canucks. Something had to give.

At times, the New Yorkers seemed to be a squad of skating zombies. Goalie Ed Giacomin's goals against average, always under 3.00, was climbing faster than the cost of living index. There were games when the graying netminder appeared to be facing ten attackers at once—including his own teammates.

"What we ought to do," scowled an exhausted Giacomin, "is call Henry Kissinger and get him to stop the bombing in our zone."

If ever the diplomacy of Henry the K was needed, it was needed now. Not only were the Rangers losing by embarrassingly lopsided scores, but that most dreaded word in sport, once only hinted at, was now being openly thrown at the Blueshirt team—dissension!

Of course, such inflammatory charges were adamantly denied by players and management, but there was more than just a bit of truth to them. The veteran checking line of Pete Stemkowski, Ted Irvine, and Bruce MacGregor had been relegated to fourth line status. The people's choice, artistic Bobby Rousseau, was gathering splinters on the bench, and then there were the trade rumors.

Pete Stemkowski, known as Stemmer to Ranger fans, has been a consistent goal scorer since coming to New York from Detroit in 1970.

"Everybody's uptight, worried about getting traded," offered Ed Giacomin. "Guys who sit out a game automatically think they're about to be traded. Guys who suddenly get to play more, think they're being showcased for a trade. It's not a good situation."

"Trade talk never helps a team," agreed redheaded Bruce MacGregor.

Even Giacomin's netminding partner, Gilles Villemure, was showing the strain. The duo of Giacomin and Villemure was generally acknowledged as the best one-two goalie tandem in the NHL. Now, with the Rangers slumping and both goaltenders yielding bushels of opposition tallies, the trade rumors had even reached their goal crease sanctuary.

"I don't know what's going on," fretted Villemure. "I've never heard so many trade rumors in my life. I don't know what my status is. He (Popein) hasn't said a word to me."

Finally, the ax did drop, and the exposed neck it fell on belonged to Glen Sather, the popular Ranger pugilist. "Slats," whose chief function was to get the Rangers' opponents' feathers ruffled, had been warming the bench lately and making his displeasure known to coach Popein.

"He hadn't been playing me since training camp," explained Sather. "I wasn't expecting to be around here much longer."

At first glance, it was a minor deal. The fiery Sather was shipped to the St. Louis Blues in return for Jack Egers, an ex-Ranger whose blistering slap shot compensated for his lack of skating finesse. Neither Sather nor Egers had been expected to answer the Rangers' problems, but Glen was one of the more popular Blueshirts, with both the fans and his teammates. His departure was seen as widening an already cavernous communications gap between Popein and the Rangers players.

Billy Fairbairn tries to carry the puck past Atlanta defenseman Pat Quinn.

Jean Ratelle has many talents—a wicked wrist shot, a fast and powerful skating style, and a keen playmaking sense.

Left wing Ted Irvine is one of the more aggressive Rangers who likes to make his presence felt, particularly against the tougher teams in the league.

Over the years, brawls between the Rangers and Boston Bruins have become familiar sights. Here, officials separate the two teams during a brawl at Madison Square Garden.

While the Rangers off ice atmosphere was, at the very least, tense, their on ice situation was downright frantic. Without a win in seven straight games, they were now confronted by the East Division-leading Boston Bruins. The game was crucial for the Blueshirts. Not only were they wallowing in sixth place, but their collective self-confidence was approaching an all-time low. A vital team meeting was called to try to clear the air.

It looked as if it was just the elixir needed. Emerging from their rap session, the Rangers miraculously seemed to have emerged from their cocoons. They stormed out to meet the Bruins. For the first time all season, the Rangers stood firm before their goalie, Ed Giacomin. The forwards back-checked fiercely and attacked in Boston's zone with a vengeance. Six different Rangers shared the wealth of scoring as the Bruins were humbled 7–3.

If some trusting foreigner visiting the United States, had, at that moment, happened to wander into Madison Square Garden, he probably would have thought he was witnessing the second coming. Horns blared, rolls of toilet paper cascaded from the balcony, fans danced in the aisles. The next day, banner newspaper headlines announced the wonder of the Rangers turnabout, confident that they were now back on the track.

But if they were, it was an up and down course that the Blueshirt elevator was taking. Even in the midst of their elation there was cause for concern. In the third period, with the Rangers ahead 6–3, Bruin defenseman Al Sims crashed into Giacomin, forcing the masked man to leave the game with a painfully twisted neck.

With Giacomin sitting out the next couple of games, the Rangers traveled south to Atlanta's Omni and a date with the hustling Atlanta Flames. After breezing to a 3–0 lead with minutes remaining in the first period, disaster almost overtook the team.

Goaltender Gilles Villemure suddenly doubled up in pain. Alarmed, teammate Dale Rolfe skated to his aid but the game little goaltender refused to be relieved. Villemure had been suffering from a slight cold before the game and was experiencing mild chest pains. He told Rolfe he would be able to make it through the first period. But as the teams were skating off the ice at the end of the frame, Gilles suffered another painful spasm.

The Flames' doctor examined the stricken netminder and ordered him to nearby Piedmont Hospital for precautionary tests.

"He scared me when he came into the dressing room," said a shaken Popein. "He suffered an attack, a severe one. He was awfully sick."

Villemure's illness, which turned out to be nothing more than the result of severe chest congestion, forced cherubic Peter McDuffe into the nets for one of his rare Ranger appearances. The New Yorkers were down to their last goaltender now, and to make an impossible situation simply unbelievable, a low slap shot by the Flames' Leon Rochefort in the opening minutes of the second period caught Peter on the unprotected part of his left ankle. The Rangers' fortunes were turning downward by the minute, but McDuffe ignored the injury and completed the game. Shaky and uncertain at first, Peter settled down and managed to hold the surging Flames to a 3–3 tie.

There were the bright sides of course, like Rod Gilbert becoming the all-time Ranger scoring leader, and a gutsy team effort that tied the tough Chicago Black Hawks late in a third period. But overall, the Blueshirts could not get a consistent streak going without a major catastrophe occurring to hinder progress.

On November 15, the Rangers traveled to Boston with visions of that 7–3 score at the Garden dancing in their heads. When they finally managed to drag themselves out of Boston Garden, they had netted two goals to the Bruins 10! The Rangers had been disgraceful. Ed Giacomin had been left on his own against Boston's heavy artillery and by the third period, Eddie's attitude seemed to be, "Oh, what's the use!"

Ranger goalie Gilles Villemure is down and severely shaken up after colliding with Chicago's Dennis Hull.

Goalie Ed Giacomin sprawls on the ice in an attempt to stop a scoring effort by California's Stan Weir.

Billy Fairbairn is very solid on his feet, one of the toughest men in the league to knock over.

The gloves are down and the fists are up during a scuffle between the Rangers and Buffalo Sabres.

Goalie Gilles Villemure stops a dangerous rolling puck on the Ranger doorstep.

Adding insult to injury, and to further complicate the Rangers' problems, center Gene Carr and forward Mike Murphy were involved in an auto accident after the game, when their taxi smashed into a Boston police car.

Both players emerged from the wreck with minor injuries, but it was an ominous foreshadowing of things to come. Two weeks later Murphy, left wing Tommy Williams, and defenseman Sheldon Kannegiesser were traded to the Los Angeles Kings for defenseman Gilles Marotte and winger Real Lemieux. Carr, once called the Ranger hope for the future, followed the trio to Los Angeles as part of a later deal.

Marotte was the key to the trade for the Rangers. An earth-shaking bodychecker, the veteran "Captain Crunch" was desperately needed to help stabilize a sieve-like Ranger defense that had been further decimated by a nagging injury to the lanky Dale Rolfe.

The Rangers were giving up gobs of goals, but thankfully, had not lost the scoring touch. True, their defense was never so porous and the usually overpowering trio of Walter Tkaczuk, Bill Fairbairn, and Steve Vickers was mired in an unexplainable scoring drought, but the lesser lights on the team were picking up the slack. The Rangers stormed into the month of December riding the crest of a ten game unbeaten streak.

During this happy period, Giacomin moved into the number one spot as the all-time Ranger shutout king, but statistics are often deceiving. Only once during the ten game streak did the Blueshirts conquer a playoff-bound club, downing the Toronto Maple Leafs 6–4. Other stops along the way included baseball-like scores such as Rangers 7–Buffalo 6, and Rangers 5–Los Angeles 5.

The Blueshirt's curious inconsistency against first division teams began to show. Buffalo, a nasty thorn in the Rangers' side in the goals against average department, all season long, walloped the New Yorkers 8–4.

Gilles Marotte lunges in front of an attacker in an attempt to poke the puck away.

Coach Popein was livid at the lack of defensive hockey. "Sure we're scoring a lot of goals," he fumed. "Damn it, we'd better start concentrating on playing some defense. Hell, we scored four this time and that should have been enough to win."

Giacomin, shaken, when five of thirteen second period shots eluded him, was replaced by Gilles Villemure.

"For Christ's sake," implored Popein. "It was enough to destroy a man's confidence the way we let Eddie down. It's not his fault when he has to try to stop two, three or four shots at a clip. Guys just stood around."

The usually subdued Popein had good reason to risk having his expletives deleted. Of course he had to feel for his goalie, but he also had to think of self-preservation, a tricky art to master if you happen to be an NHL coach—and a losing coach at that. The season was more than one-third over and the Rangers were clinging precariously to third place. Worse yet, was the fact that in their twelve games with playoff-bound clubs, the Ranger record stood at a sickly two wins, five losses and five ties—nine points out of a possible 24.

There would be encouraging signs, to be sure, like clutch, come-from-behind goals to tie Buffalo and Toronto. But then there were the horrendous, landslide losses. A 6–1 massacre at the hands of the Chicago Black Hawks; a 7–1 nightmare at the Montreal Forum; and a 4–2 loss to the Boston Bruins on national television that saw the Rangers waste an early 2–0 lead.

"It's gotten to the point," said a frustrated Ted Irvine, "where we've forgotten how to win."

"We stopped hitting, quit being aggressive," said Popein, vainly searching for answers to his teams' haplessness. "We couldn't get the fellows to hit hard after we got the two goals. I don't know why. It can be a psychological thing that just happens."

Ted Irvine's summation was much more chilling. "Not all 20 guys on this team are pulling together," was his blunt evaluation.

*Ted Irvine surrounded by Black Hawks
as everyone awaits the face-off.*

Walt Tkaczuk congratulates Steve Vickers after the left wing scores against the New York Islanders.

The puck is just beyond the reach of Billy Fairbairn as the California goalie challenges the Ranger wing.

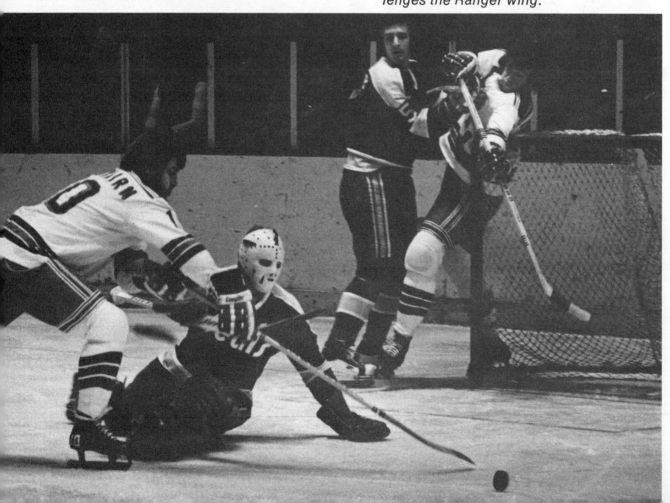

Gilles Villemure puts his pads in the way
of the puck before the attacker can score.

Ted Irvine barrels past a Seal defender
and shoots the puck toward the California
net.

Rod Seiling is one of the most dependable defensemen in the NHL.

Dale Rolfe tries to get by an enemy attacker.

the return
of the cat

Under the leadership of Emile "The Cat" Francis the Rangers made the playoffs for eight consecutive years through 1974.

Just six days later, on January 10, 1974, following a shocking 7–2 butchering at the hands of the Buffalo Sabres, Larry Popein was relieved of his duties as Ranger coach. For the third time in his up again-down again coaching career, Emile Francis replaced an incumbent coach in mid-season.

Emile grudgingly assumed the reins in what amounted to a last resort move. It registered on the Rangers' players' psyche that the Cat meant business.

"We know if we don't start producing now," stated Brad Park, "someone else will be leaving and it won't be Emile."

"I'm going to crack down on these guys," vowed an enraged Francis after the Buffalo massacre. "We'd better make the playoffs, and you can underline the word better."

Francis had good reason for his disgust. The Rangers, as a team, simply had not put out for coach Popein. Several players had hinted at this outrage, and his leaving hardly caused any remorse among the Blueshirts.

Instead, there was an endless stream of rationalizations.

"It's a human thing," said Rod Gilbert, trying to explain why a group of professionals found it so hard to play for their coach. "Francis understands us and we understand him. It's really his team because he brought us all together. He can relate to us and we can relate to him. He can tell us we're playing awful and do it in a way that doesn't make us mad."

"Coaches are like servants today," offered Bobby Rousseau. And who could argue with him; a major problem could have been that Popein's salary as Ranger coach was a mere pittance compared to the paychecks some of his players picked up every two weeks.

"They've got to do more than coach," Bobby continued. "They've got to know what to say to the players, and how to say it."

"There was no communication between us," said Ted Irvine of the departed coach. "No life at all."

Steve Vickers had a simpler explanation. "Popein," said the goal-scoring boy wonder, "couldn't scare us." Francis, he felt, could.

Emile had not wanted to relieve Popein; he had tried to maintain as low a profile as possible during the first half of the season, leaving the responsibility for team direction up to his heir. It just had not worked.

It has been said of all professional athletes that they are basically immature, making their grown-up livelihood playing children's games. The Rangers had demonstrated this by rebelling against the new teacher, tormenting the new baby-sitter, but when Mother Cat Emile returned home, they all sat up straight and swore they'd never do it again. It was, however, no way for professionals to behave and people were pointing to Francis, blaming him for coddling his players.

Bobby Rousseau in action against the California Golden Seals.

Bruce MacGregor tries to steal the puck
from Phil Esposito of Boston.

Ted Irvine enjoyed his best season in 1973-74 netting 25 goals and collecting 20 assists for 45 points.

Dale Rolfe dumps a Pittsburgh Penguin who intruded on Ranger ice.

True, Francis did build the Rangers from a hapless group of sixth place skaters to consistent Stanley Cup challengers, but there seemed to be a lack of desire or motivation that clouded Francis-coached Ranger teams. Some feel that he is too much an organization man. Emile developed strong loyalties with certain players. The players, in turn, felt that they could do no wrong.

Francis' firm belief in "Ranger people" is what prompted him to name Popein to the coaching post in the first place.

"He had been with us in the organization for five years," said Francis of Popein, "and it was only fair that I gave him the first opportunity."

All the while, it was common knowledge in the NHL inner circles that Popein had had communication problems with his players when he was coaching at Providence. Francis chose to ignore this because of his fierce loyalty to organization men, reasoning that things would be different in the big leagues.

With the painful Popein era behind them, Francis and the Rangers now set to the task of making the playoffs. They did, finishing the season locked in third place.

The Rangers played winning hockey for Emile, chalking up a 22–10–5 record. This was good enough to get them into the playoffs, but their record against first division teams was still a far cry from that of a serious Cup contender. Even under the spiritual guidance of a Francis, the Rangers managed a so-so record of 7–6–3 against the top clubs.

Their road record left much to be desired and as the season wound down to its final stages, the Blueshirts won only one of their final seven road games, yielding an incredible thirty-five goals in that span.

With this sort of encouragement, the Rangers warily entered the first round of the Stanley Cup Playoffs.

Steve Vickers flicks the puck past St. Louis goalie John Davidson.

Ted Irvine prepares to land a right punch on an opposing skater as the official lets both players fight it out.

Larry Sacharuk saw limited action with the Rangers in 1973-74.

Jerry Butler showed promising signs during his 1973-74 rookie season. Here he tries to poke the puck away from Chicago's Doug Jarrett.

Brad Park, considered by many observers as the NHL's number two defenseman after Bobby Orr, is a consistent scorer and a hard checker.

Goalie Ed Giacomin comes out to cut down
Stan Mikita's shooting angle.

another quest

Goalie Ed Giacomin makes a save on a shot by a Montreal invader.

The first playoff hurdle for the Rangers in their 1974 quest for the Stanley Cup was the Montreal Canadiens. The Rangers had won only two of the six regular season meetings between the clubs, dropping three on Forum ice. The outlook was bleak as the New Yorkers traveled north for the first two games of the series.

But lo and behold—the Rangers whipped Montreal, 4–1, in the first game and returned to Madison Square Garden with a split and a possible "break service" in the home ice advantage department.

There was one pesky little problem—Yvan Cournoyer. With a little help from his friend, Steve Shutt, and goaltender Michel (Bunny) Larocque, Cournoyer almost single-handedly dazzled the New Yorkers 4–2 in the third game and put Montreal up two games to one.

Bruce MacGregor was a favorite with Madison Square Garden fans. One of the quickest and most elusive skaters in the league, MacGregor is a hardworking and hard checking player either at center or in his normal slot on the right side.

Another loss would mean curtains for the Blueshirts and they knew it. The speedy skating of Cournoyer and Shutt had downed the Rangers. Only the acrobatics of Eddie Giacomin prevented an all-out rout by the Canadiens. Drastic measures were needed, and Eddie delivered them.

Showing a flair for the dramatic in the locker room as well as between the pipes, Giacomin seized the bull by the horns. In a move calculated to rally the sagging troops, Eddie flew into a rage at questioning newsmen following the third game. Staunchly defending his mates, Giacomin accused the media of being a bunch of overly critical, nit-picking muckrakers. He must have been doing something right—it worked.

There were other aspects, of course; the Rangers had to win three more hockey games, but the record speaks for itself. After Eddie's tirade, the Rangers proceeded, in dramatic fashion, to whip the suspenders off the Canadiens.

With the hardworking Bruce MacGregor assigned to stay in Cournoyer's hip pocket wherever he might roam, the roadrunning Hab was not heard from again. "Cousin Brucie" even found time in his labors to score four goals himself, including a heart-stopping tally with twelve seconds remaining in game five, to force it into overtime.

It took only four minutes into the extra session for Pete Stemkowski to shovel a face-off back to Ron Harris, another of the Rangers unsung-turned-hero. Harris didn't hesitate an instant as he sent a rising blur into the far corner of the net. The Rangers had won the fifth game and now led in the series three games to two.

"Before the game I called my wife and told her if the game went into overtime, I'd score the winning goal," said Harris, basking in his unfamiliar role as a scorer. "She told me I was a liar. She had a point, too, because I got only two goals all season."

66

"His job is to rattle bones," said admiring coach Francis of the rock-hard Harris. "He skates in a straight line and hits everything in his way. He makes things happen."

Things were happening all right. Incredibly, the Rangers had shed their regular season sheepishness and were seriously threatening the defending Stanley Cup champions with elimination. Strangest of all was the fact that it was the likes of Harris, MacGregor, Stemkowski and Irvine, bit players in the Rangers' star-studded cast, who were providing the punch.

The scene shifted to Madison Square Garden for the sixth game and, following the pattern of the entire series, the Canadiens quickly took a 2–0 lead. But things were different now; there was no panic, no urgency. No longer were the Rangers the group of frantic, disorganized skaters they had been through much of the regular campaign.

None other than Bruce MacGregor flashed to the goalmouth, neatly faked Larocque out of position and scored—the Rangers were on the board. Now, the higher-tax-bracket Rangers got down to business. Steve Vickers, drawing Larocque out of his net, slid a tantalizingly slow pass to linemate Bill Fairbairn who chipped the puck into the wide open net to tie the score. Then it was the combination of Gilbert and Jean Ratelle who repeated the act in the third period, Jean converting Rod's pass and the Rangers were ahead to stay.

Just so he wouldn't be forgotten, Pete Stemkowski scored two goals into the empty net to pound the final nail in the Habitants' coffin. There was pandemonium and delirium. Two short weeks before it had been unthinkable but the Rangers had really beaten Montreal and would advance to the semifinals against the brash, brawling Philadelphia Flyers.

Vic Hadfield a thirteen year veteran with the Blueshirts, was traded to the Pittsburgh Penguins after the 1973-74 season.

Dale Rolfe and Montreal's Murray Wilson exchange punches during a contest at Madison Square Garden.

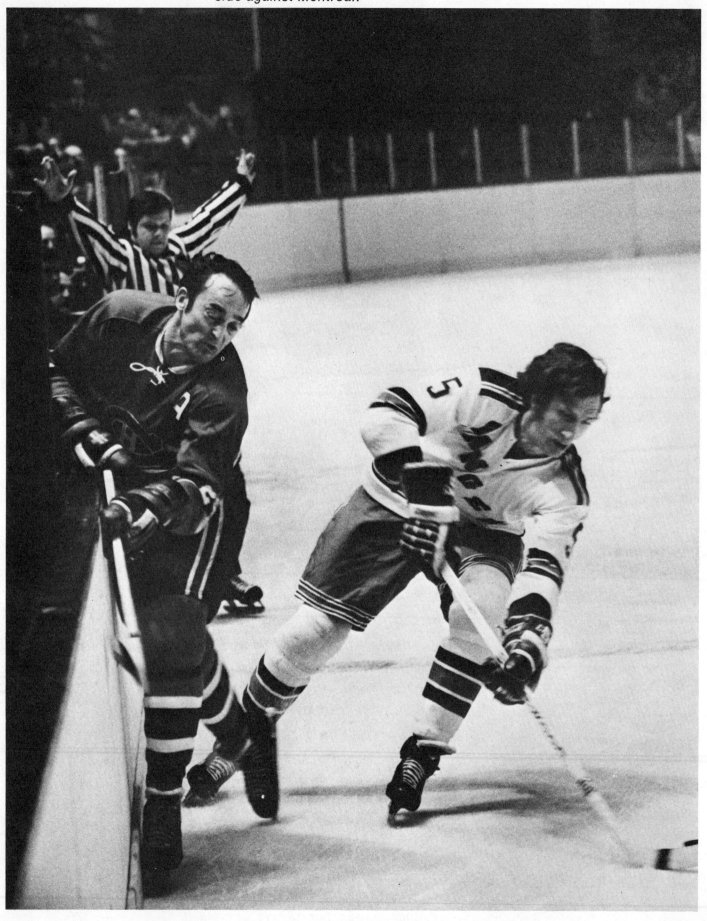

Dale Rolfe carries the puck down the right side against Montreal.

Goalie Gilles Villemure watches as the puck goes wide of the net.

Steve Vickers carries the puck up ice against the Montreal Canadiens.

facing the flyers

The Flyers had finished first in the NHL West on the strength of the superb goaltending of Bernie Parent, the artistry of their two fine young centers, Bobby Clarke and Rick MacLeish, and the not so subtle tactics of Messrs. Schultz, Kelly, Dupont, et al. But, the Rangers reasoned, after all, Philadelphia was only an expansion team. The New Yorkers had learned long ago to grow fat at the expense of expansionists.

The Rangers' book on the Flyers was simple; play your normal game, don't be intimidated, and by the third period, class will tell. The Flyers, they crowed, surely can fight, but simply can't skate with the New York Rangers.

There was an added incentive for the New Yorkers, too. The Flyers had made quick work of their quarter-final opponents, the surprising Atlanta Flames, in four straight games, and then turned their attention to the still-raging duel between the Rangers and Canadiens. When the Brotherly Love sextet was asked which of the two teams they'd rather face in the semifinals, Dave Schultz was quick to stand up and deliver a well-aimed barb at the Rangers.

With Flyer Bill Barber down, Vic Hadfield (11) and Walt Tkaczuk prepare to launch a rush up ice.

"I'd like to play the Rangers because they have a reputation of choking in the past," he stated bluntly. Immediately, Schultz's quote became Topic A on the Ranger bulletin board.

"Well, they haven't done well against us before, have they?" asked Rod Gilbert.

"I'm happy for Schultz," said Ted Irvine. "He got what he wanted, the chance to play us."

"Mr. Schultz must figure he's one of the all-time greats," sneered Emile Francis. "We'll take care of his quotes and then they can be put in the Hall of Fame."

If the Rangers were sounding a bit cocky, no one could really blame them. The New Yorkers had met the Flyers five times during the regular season, winning two and tying two against only one loss.

Jean Ratelle voiced the sentiments of his teammates as the Rangers traveled to Philly for the first two games of the series. Never given to wordiness, Ratelle was direct and to the point. "We're good enough to beat them," was Jean's evaluation. Everyone seemed to agree. Except, of course, the Flyers.

Flyers' coach Fred Shero had his own plans tucked up his sleeve. Always an innovator, Shero is the type of coach who searches endlessly for an edge. He knew, along with almost every knowledgeable NHL observer, that, on paper, the Rangers were clearly superior to his Flyers. The goaltending, a crucial key in any short series, was just about even, with Giacomin holding a slight advantage. Eddie's edge was his ability to handle the puck, either clearing it out of danger or headmanning it up to spring the attack. Philadelphia, on the other hand, had young legs, with an average age of 26 to the Rangers' 30.

Shero decided that Giacomin's roaming, a big factor in the downfall of the Canadiens, had to be stopped. He vowed that his bigger skaters would "use the body" if they had to.

"If we have to take a penalty," said the thinking man's coach, "the whole world will know about it."

Goalie Ed Giacomin dives on a loose puck in front of the net.

It was obvious what Freddie Shero and the Flyers had in mind from the very first game in Philadelphia. Whenever Giacomin would roam from his crease, a pesky Flyer would corral him against the board or pin him to the side of the net. The Philadelphians, most notably Gary Dornhoefer, also set up shop just outside Eddie's goal area, giving the beleaguered netminder an excellent view of several orange and black derrieres, but not a very good panorama of the ice.

Eddie was the first to attest to the effectiveness of the tactic.

"Dornhoefer is one of the best in the league at screening and interfering with the goalie," said Giacomin in bitter admiration. "I kept yelling at the ref, but what can I do?"

Eddie couldn't do much against the Flyers in that first game. He was spectacular in defeat, but was almost callously left unprotected by his defensemen. The 4–0 Ranger humiliation set a pattern that would hold throughout the series with clockwork precision. The Rangers' defensemen inexplicably chose to ignore the Flyers' invasion of their goalkeeper's sanctuary. Realizing his plight, Eddie took the matter into his own hands, venturing far out of his net to clear the puck. This, too, backfired when Ross Lonsberry hog-tied Giacomin against the boards and Rick MacLeish gleefully deposited the puck into the vacated cage.

The Rangers were concerned, but not desperate— not yet. Shero's swirling, European hockey tactics had the Rangers baffled. The net hangers had them bewildered, and all that was left was for Schultz & Co. to bully them.

Francis wanted to make sure that the latter would never happen, so he inserted his Dead End Kid, Jerry "Bugsy" Butler at right wing in place of the mild-mannered Bruce MacGregor. Unfortunately for Butler, it was none other than Bob (Hound) Kelly who was manning the left wing slot for Philadelphia. The two teams were lined up for a face-off when Butler glanced over his shoulder at his opposite number. That was all the incentive Kelly needed. In one quick swoop, Kelly was all

Jerry Butler enjoyed a fine rookie season with the Rangers in 1973-74.

Rod Seiling one of the better stickhandling defensemen, carries the puck out of his zone.

Gilles Villemure prepares to make a save.

over Butler, right crosses flying. The Hound was victor in a unanimous decision, and after only nineteen seconds of the game, the tone of the contest had been firmly established.

The Rangers were so thoroughly disorganized and bewildered in the second game, it was only fitting that the crucial call of the night be against them. Midway through the second period with the Flyers leading 1–0 on a first period goal by Bobby Clarke, the Philadelphians were chasing the puck deep in the New York end. Harried by the pesky fore-checking of Ross Lonsberry, Ranger defenseman Gilles Marotte took a desperate golf-style whack at the puck, trying to clear it out of danger.

Suddeny, Philly blueliner Ed Van Impe intercepted the rubber just before it bounced out to center ice and flipped a soft shot in the general direction of the Rangers' goal. Rod Seiling, trying to control the bouncing disk, watched in horror as it took an uncanny hop off his stick and flew straight up at Ed Giacomin. Realizing that the puck was beginning to roll down his arm and into the net, Giacomin hit the ice immediately, apparently trapping the puck under his body before it crossed the goal line.

The Flyers, of course, raised their sticks in triumph, believing the puck had gone in. The referee, Dave Newell, had not been in position to make the call and was skating behind the net to confer with the goal judge when the red light went on. The goal judge had awarded the score to Philadelphia.

A disbelieving Ed Giacomin exploded. He barreled behind his net, pounding at the glass-partitioned goal judge's seat. The cords of his neck stood out like highways on a roadmap as he vainly tried to plead his case. But, referees are the only people who win hockey arguments, so the goal stood.

"I swear on a stack of Bibles that that puck did not go over the line," said Eddie after the game, still highly emotional over the disastrous call.

Of course the goal judge, an official assigned from the neutral city of St. Louis, believed he had made the correct judgment.

Vic Hadfield plants himself in front of the Philadelphia net to screen out Flyer goalie Bernie Parent.

"I saw the puck completely over the line," said the lamplighter, "and I pushed the goal button."

Giacomin had to be removed from the game briefly to regain his composure, but that goal had taken all the wind out of the Rangers' sails. The New Yorkers got two goals to make it respectable, but the Flyers had won the first two games, and in convincing fashion. The scene shifted to Madison Square Garden for games three and four and the New Yorkers had to start making things happen again.

Needing someone to stand up to the Philly ruffians, Captain Vic Hadfield was suited up for the third contest. Hadfield had been sidelined since the third Montreal game with a painful turned ankle, but now the Rangers had their backs to the wall. Vic was a welcome addition to the thin ranks of Rangers' heavy hitters as both teams came out battling. A whopping total of 109 minutes in penalties were dished out in the game, with the main attractions being heavyweight bouts between Dave Schultz and Brad Park, Gary Dornhoefer and Steve Vickers, and Rick MacLeish and Park. The fisticuffs ended in a tie, but the Rangers, after trailing 2–0, came back strong to win the game 5–3 and trail in the series two games to one.

"We were down 2–0 and 3–1 and we said to ourselves, 'Hey, what the hell is going on?'" recounted Brad Park. "It was a time we could have panicked. We didn't panic, we played good, steady hockey."

Brad's steadiness resulted in the Rangers' winning goal. Ted Irvine and Rod Gilbert ganged up on Barry Ashbee behind the Flyer net, forcing him to cough up the puck. Gilbert snared it and threw the rubber out to Park who had followed the play in deep.

"I took one whack at it, I took another whack at it, then it was in," said Park beaming. Rod Gilbert added another insurance score and the Rangers were back in the series.

"We were guilty of not retaliating in the first two games," admitted Steve Vickers, author of the Rangers' second goal. "Tonight we did and won."

Walter Tkaczuk in action against Philadelphia. Tkaczuk wore the football-type
helmet to protect his wired jaw, injured
weeks earlier.

A stick save is made by Ed Giacomin.

Rod Seiling, a scrappy Ranger defense-man, is sprawled on the ice.

"We didn't start the fights," chimed in Park with a toothless smile, "but we sure as hell participated in them."

The hobbling Hadfield, his mobility severely hampered, managed to counter the tough going around the net and slam the tying goal past Parent. He paid for his marker though, as he was checked by Van Impe on the scoring play, reinjuring his already tender ankle, and leaving the game.

Not only were the Blueshirts scoring, they started to dish out some body checks rather than receiving them. Steady Ron Harris, whose stiff hip check had TKO'd the Boston Bruins' scoring machine, Phil Esposito, in the previous season's playoffs, repeated the act with a crisp upending of bad boy Kelly. The result: severely strained knee ligaments and Kelly was lost for the remainder of the playoffs.

The Rangers had even found the gumption to invade Bernie Parent's crease, a la Dornhoefer. On Hadfield's scoring play, Vic was a Rock of Gibraltar, holding his ground just to the left of Parent. When Rod Gilbert's goalmouth pass slid toward the crease, Hadfield lunged for the puck, smashing into Parent and deflecting the rubber into the net.

Parent suffered a bruised thigh on that play, but if it was bothering him at all, it certainly didn't show in the fourth game of the series. Parent was brilliant, and in the Rangers' goal, Giacomin was his equal.

After a barrage of outrage was aired over the viciousness that marked the third game, the fourth contest was relatively tame. The Flyers' Joe Watson scored in the first period to put Philadelphia ahead 1–0, and judging from Parent's performance in the Flyers' net, it looked like it could very well stay that way for the remainder of the game.

But at the eighteen minute mark of the second period, the black rubber disk began to bounce for the Rangers. Brad Park had the puck in the Flyers' zone and dumped it off to Jean Ratelle. Bobby Rousseau, skating in place of Hadfield, burst into the open and Jean laid the puck on his stick. The artful Bobby flipped the puck at Parent. Bernie lunged and deflected the puck with his stick. The rubber squirted straight up, arched over Parent's shoulder, and landed just outside the goal line.

Former Ranger captain Vic Hadfield and Rod Gilbert on the prowl against Philadelphia.

Walt Tkaczuk and Philadelphia's Ed Van Impe have words at the Flyers' net.

Pete Stemkowski dumps Philadelphia's Orest Kindrachuk during 1974 playoff action.

The goal judge, now showed the Flyers the other side of the coin and turned the red light on for the Blueshirts, ruling that on its downward arc, the puck had crossed the goal line. The Flyers put up a halfhearted protest, but the goal stood. Now the score was tied at 1–1.

It was still tied 1–1 when the buzzer sounded ending regulation play. After a brief intermission, the teams returned to the ice for overtime. The Rangers desperately needed this game. If they lost, they would return to Philadelphia for the fifth game, down 3–1. Both teams played it cautiously at first, waiting for a break.

Ed Giacomin fell to his knees to make an artful save on the dangerous MacLeish. The Ranger defense corralled the puck and cleared it out to center ice, trying for a forward line change. Jean Ratelle and Bobby Rousseau scurried to the bench and were replaced by Walt Tkazcuk and Steve Vickers. Rod Gilbert, expecting to be relieved by Bill Fairbairn, started for the Ranger bench when suddenly, Tkazcuk intercepted an errant Flyer pass and quickly headmanned it to Steve Vickers. Steve, standing at the left point, was startled to see Gilbert reverse his field and instinctively break for the net.

Instantly, Vickers unleashed a shot toward the far corner of the cage. The puck, Gilbert, and Parent arrived at the same point at the same time and something had to give. It was Parent who gave way. The puck squirted through his legs and the Rangers had miraculously pulled it off. For the second time in the playoffs, the Rangers had come from behind to win in overtime. What was developing into a home-ice series now moved back to the unfriendly confines of the Philadelphia Spectrum.

Inexplicably the Rangers seemed to lose their killer instinct in the foreign arena. Pete Stemkowski put the Rangers on the scoreboard early in the first period, but that was it for the New York offense. The Blueshirts squandered six power play opportunities, including two that saw the Philadelphians with only three skaters on the ice. And then, there was the irrepressible Mr. Dornhoefer again. His net hanging tactics tormented Giacomin throughout the game while Rangers' defensemen seemed to look the other way. With Eddie Giacomin

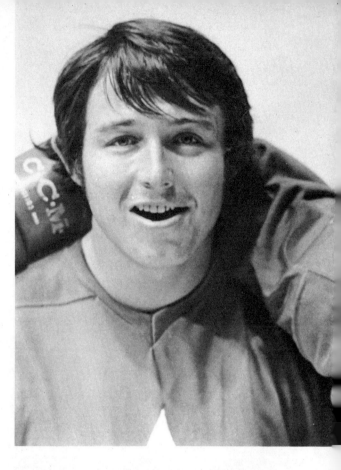

Brad Park and right wing Rod Gilbert both participated in the Team Canada-Russia series in 1972.

Bobby Rousseau came to the Rangers in 1971 from Minnesota in exchange for Bob Nevin. He has displayed great speed and flashy stickhandling throughout his NHL career.

frantically trying to clear Dorny out of his line of vision, Rick MacLeish fired a leisurely thirty-footer into the short side of the net for the winning goal. The Flyers added two more tallies and rolled to a 4–1 victory.

And now, after shaking off their regular season doldrums, after defeating the favored Canadiens in the quarterfinals, the Rangers were facing elimination at the hands of the Flyers.

"There will be changes," said a tight-lipped Emile Francis after the loss that put his club down three games to two.

"Anyone who can walk will probably play. We've got to do something about our power play," he continued, but that was obvious. What was even more obvious was Francis' next statement. "All I know is that we can't lose any more games."

With this grim knowledge, the atmosphere in Madison Square Garden was filled with tension as the sixth game got underway. Like boxers, each team felt the other out at the start, trying to establish dominance, but Giacomin and Parent were as impenetrable as ever. Then, with a little more than five minutes gone in the first period, Don Saleski sneaked behind the Ranger defense, faked Giacomin to his knees, and deposited the puck in the open corner of the net. Saleski's burst had seemed so effortless and free of Ranger interference, that it appeared the home ice advantage might cease to be a factor, at least for the Rangers.

Bolstered by their one goal lead, the Flyers pressed the attack and once again began to take liberties with Giacomin. Eddie decided the time had come to settle this matter once and for all.

It was Ross Lonsberry who was cramping Eddie's style, when the masked man lashed out at his tormentor with his heavy goalie stick. Lonsberry had the unmitigated gall to try to discuss Eddie's actions with him and received a goalie glove in his face. Giacomin drew a double minor penalty for his rowdiness, but at least he had staked out his territory. The Flyers steered clear of his net for the remainder of the game and when a foolhardy Philadelphian was absent minded enough to wander a bit too close, a firm rap against his ankles quickly reminded him of Eddie's militancy.

Inspired by his goaltender's spunk, the sharpshooting Park promptly knocked down a Flyers' clearing pass at the blue line and shot a 45-footer past Parent. The Flyers and Rangers exchanged thrusts, time and time again, only to be thwarted by the two netminders. Both clubs played absolutely airtight defense and the score remained tied at one goal apiece. Late in the second period, Flyers' captain Bobby Clarke took a bank pass from teammate Bill Barber, got behind the Ranger defense, and had Giacomin one-on-one. Coming out to meet the Philly sharpshooter, Eddie sprawled, barely managing to deflect the puck up over the glass and out of play. Clarke was left staring at the empty net, shaking his head.

"I had room on top of the net," said Clarke after the game. "Three times before, Giacomin stopped me when I shot it on the ice. This time I wanted to go high on him."

He did, but Eddie got a piece of it. That save turned out to be the pivotal point of the game.

The third period began with the teams still deadlocked at one goal each. Then, four minutes into the final stanza, Dale Rolfe spotted Ron Harris free from his check, along the right boards. Dale fired the puck to the sturdy Harris as Flyer Bruce Cowick bore down on him. Ronnie brought the puck into the Flyers' zone and from an almost impossible angle, snapped off a deceptive wrist shot. Parent, surprised at the suddenness of the shot, was handcuffed. The puck flew toward him and hit the corner of the net. The Rangers were ahead 2–1 and were coming alive.

Less than two minutes later, Ted Irvine emerged from a scramble in front of the net and nudged the puck goalward. Parent, who was down on the ice and out of position when the rubber squirted free, stabbed futilely at the puck as it trickled lazily over the goal line. Vickers added another score into the vacated net in the game's last moments and the series was tied at three games apiece, forcing a decisive seventh game in Philadelphia.

Ed Giacomin had been brilliant. Ron Harris' heroics evoked sweet anticipation of a repeat of the Montreal series. The Rangers were confident they could finally break the frustrating hex of Philadelphia's Spectrum.

Left wing Ted Irvine and Philadelphia's Barry Ashbee await a face-off.

Forward Billy Fairbairn is considered one of the best penalty killers in the NHL.

Ed Giacomin spots one puck that got away during a contest with the Philadelphia Flyers.

only a goal away

Ted Irvine with the puck.

"Maybe we should hope they do get the first goal," kidded Bill Fairbairn. "We seem to play better and win after we give up the first goal."

It was true enough. All three Ranger wins had seen the Blueshirts come back from early 1–0 deficits.

Not only were the Rangers battling the Flyers and the Spectrum jinx, but they also had the Flyers' powerful good luck talisman, Kate Smith's recording of "God Bless America" to contend with.

The Rangers scored first with Bill Fairbairn, himself, netting the go-ahead mark. However, less than a minute after Fairbairn's marker, Bobby Clarke passed the puck from a maze of players to an unguarded Rick MacLeish who rifled it into the open side of the net, tying the score.

Hard work by Orest Kindrachuck, Ross Lonsberry, and Gary Dornhoefer resulted in two unanswered Philly goals in the second period. Was there no stopping Miss Smith's magic? The Rangers entered the third period trailing 3–1.

Parent, like some mystical masked wizard, blunted every surge the Rangers could muster until a determined Steve Vickers finally slammed the puck past him at 8:49 of the final period.

Realizing that their season might be over in 10 short minutes, the Rangers were desperately trying to reverse the trend. It was almost a certainty that they would now tie the game.

The Flyers were feeling the pressure and started to press. Forty-nine seconds after Vickers' goal Ross Lonsberry flicked the puck in front of the Ranger net where a waiting Dornhoefer pounced on it and drilled it over Giacomin and into the cage. The Rangers were dazed. Once again they were down by two goals. Even though Dornhoefer's second goal had shaken the New York skaters, they still pressed the attack. With five-and-one-half minutes remaining in the game, Pete Stemkowski took Vickers' pass and backhanded a bullet beyond Parent. Now the score was 4–3. Could the Rangers ask yet another miracle from their weary skaters?

The seconds ticked away with the Rangers trying desperately for the equalizer. Memories of Bruce MacGregor's clutch goal with seconds remaining against Montreal glistened in their memories. Now there was less than one minute remaining. Giacomin virtually flew to the Ranger bench to allow a sixth skater to join the fray. Don Saleski frantically snared the puck and shot it the length of the ice to relieve the pressure.

The New Yorkers got back to touch the puck and linesman John D'Amico blew the whistle for icing; or so the Rangers thought.

But no, it wasn't icing! D'Amico had detected the sixth Rangers' skater leaving the bench area before Giacomin had left the ice. D'Amico had called a two-minute penalty on the Rangers for having too many men on the ice. The Rangers were sunk.

Rangers captain Vic Hadfield who was traded to Pittsburgh after the season, was named to serve the two minute bench penalty. Helplessly, Vic was forced to watch the last excruciating seconds of the Ranger season from the penalty box as the Flyers skated their way to victory.

General manger-coach Emile Francis could not find words for his grief and disappointment. "We went down swinging," were the only consoling sentiments he could offer.

What went wrong? It might be said that this was the year the Rangers, as a team, finally grew old. It might be said that they had become fat and complacent.

Really, it was the difference of just one goal and a penalty that was so bizarre in its suddenness, that it almost didn't belong. The Rangers had played well in the seventh game, well enough to win. Does one goal make a season?

Ed Giacomin knocks the puck away from the goal with his leg pads.

Bruce MacGregor came to the Rangers from Detroit in 1971. The swift-skating right wing jumped to Edmonton of the World Hockey Association in 1974.

Bobby Rousseau faces off.

Walt Tkaczuk holds his ground against Larry Robinson of Montreal.

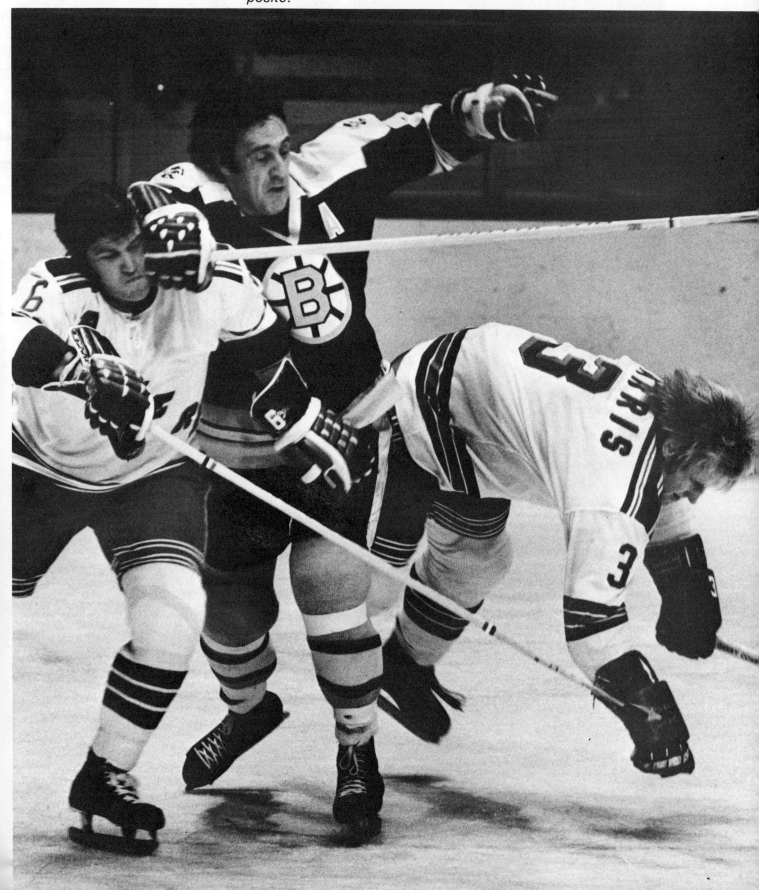

Defensemen Gilles Marotte (6) and Ron Harris (3) combine to sandwich Phil Esposito.

Steve Vickers has a wide open Bruin net to shoot at with goalie Gilles Gilbert out of position.

the present and future rangers

eddie giacomin

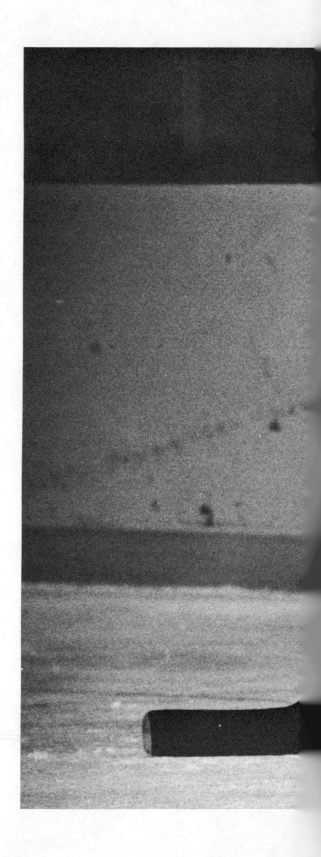

Even if it is against NHL rules for a goalie to be captain, one must realize that more than anything else, a captain is supposed to be the undisputed team leader. And it was none other than the graying Giacomin who personally rallied the New Yorkers against the brash Philadelphia Flyers in the 1974 Stanley Cup semifinals.

Eddie was simply fantastic against the bullyboys, blocking shots, clearing the puck, and keeping—or trying to keep—his crease free of Flyers. But the highest praise paid to the masked man came from his opponents—the Flyers themselves.

"He played his guts out against us and he lost." said Terry Crisp, one of the hardest working Flyers. "I think every guy on our club came out of the series with great respect for Giacomin."

Eddie Giacomin is the Rangers' first string goalie. He shared the Vezina Trophy with Gilles Villemure in 1970-71.

Goalie Ed Giacomin frequently comes out of his net to clear the puck from the Ranger zone.

When the Ranger defense seemed to show reluctance in dislodging Flyers roadblocks from Eddie's turf, Giacomin took charge of the situation by throwing his own weight around the goalmouth. He whacked Ross Lonsberry, shoved Don Saleski, and poked Gary Dornhoefer. He refused to be intimidated.

Eddie also found the time to put on the best display of goaltending in his playoff career. Many observers pointed to Flyers' goalie, Bernie Parent, as the semifinal round's outstanding player, and Parent *was* superb. But all he had to do was tend goal, not clear the puck and fight off his tormentors.

Eddie had given it his best. He was spectacular throughout both Rangers' playoff series but was beaten by just one goal. It was a tough playoff for the battling senior statesman of the Rangers. It had been a tough season, too.

For the first time since his nightmarish rookie season, Eddie's goals against average was above three goals per game. The Rangers as a team surrendered their highest total of enemy tallies in 30 years. When this starts happening to a hockey club, no matter how unjustly, the goalie usually gets the blame.

Playing in 56 regular season games, Eddie was a workhorse for the New Yorkers in 1973-74. During the playoffs, his netminding partner, Gilles Villemure saw only a few brief seconds of action while Eddie cooled off after violently protesting a disputed Flyer goal.

In all, 168 pucks flew past Giacomin during the regular campaign, giving him a slightly paunchy goals against average of 3.07—respectable, but hardly sensational. Yet, Eddie did manage to pick up five shutouts and become the all-time leading Ranger in the goose-egg department.

The captaincy would surely be fitting to Giacomin, but unless he switches positions or starts lobbying for a rule change, the chances are slim. No matter, really, the Rangers know very well where to turn for leadership when the going gets rough—they look between the pipes, to Ed Giacomin.

Rod Gilbert participated in the Team Canada-Russia series in 1972 on a line with teammate Jean Ratelle.

Rod Gilbert became the most prolific scorer in Ranger history during the 1973-74 season. By season's end Gilbert had scored 304 goals as a Ranger, breaking the old record of 272, set by Andy Bathgate.

rod gilbert

Rod Gilbert's NHL career almost ended before it really started. Playing for the Guelph Royals in the Ontario Hockey Association, he skidded on an ice-cream container top thrown to the ice by a fan, and injured his back. A few days later an opponent leveled him with a strong check, and Gilbert fell to the ice, his back broken. The first operation on his spine was a near disaster; his left leg began to hemorrhage and amputation was seriously considered. During the summer of 1965 the bone grafts in his back weakened, and another operation was needed. Rod's career was in jeopardy; he played 34 games in a restrictive brace and then submitted to another operation. Happily, Rod's story has been all uphill to fame since then.

With Jean Ratelle breaking down the left
side, right wing Rod Gilbert crosses the
red line onto enemy ice.

On February 24, 1968, at the Montreal Forum, Gilbert scored four goals against Rogatien Vachon, and also established an NHL record—16 shots on goal. In 1971-72 he hit for 40 goals, finished fifth in the NHL scoring race and was named right wing on the first All-Star team. He was the first Ranger in eight years to get a first team nomination. In 1974 Gilbert passed Andy Bathgate as the Rangers' all-time leading scorer. His milestone goal was celebrated by a five minute, deafening ovation.

He teamed with Jean Ratelle and Vic Hadfield to form the Rangers' number one line. The G-A-G line (goal-a-game) amassed 139 goals and 312 points in 1971-72. But Ratelle broke his ankle, and Rod was hindered by pinched nerves in his neck; otherwise the Rangers might have taken the Cup from the Bruins that year.

In 1973-74 Gilbert scored 35 goals and 77 points despite the Rangers' problems. He showed his deep competitive spirit as he helped the Rangers in their upward spiral from sixth to third place. Rod's dramatic overtime goal in the semifinal playoff against the Philadelphia Flyers was one of his most spectacular plays. He has always been a clutch player in that race for the Cup. Originally from Montreal, Gilbert has adjusted well to the fast-paced life of New York City and is close to the hearts of the fans. But like other Rangers, Rod Gilbert wants his name engraved on the Stanley Cup. No matter who leads the Rangers to that big prize, the pride and ability of Rod Gilbert will be important factors.

brad park

Until the day he hangs up his skates, Brad Park will not escape comparison with Bobby Orr. Although Brad takes on his "number two" role with little argument, it is obvious that Park's value to the Rangers is similar to Orr's importance to Boston. When the Rangers were in one of their numerous slumps in 1973-74, Park was almost always looked for to somehow lead the club out of the morass. In August, 1974, he became team captain.

Park's stinging slap shot from the point and outstanding stickhandling have resulted in two twenty-goal seasons. In 1971 he turned the hat trick twice against the Pittsburgh Penguins.

Brad came up through Toronto's minor hockey leagues. He joined the Rangers' training camp in 1968, and modestly predicted that "I'm going to be the third defenseman on this team."

Park showed his willingness to hit in his rookie season when he confronted Mr. Hockey himself, Gordie Howe. Park crunched his 190 pounds into Howe's gut, but the next thing he remembers is Rangers' trainer Frank Paice leaning over him with smelling salts. Any other rookie would have wisely turned away, but Park showed the cockiness that has made him the team leader. He went up to Howe and said calmly, "One more like that and this stick goes down your throat."

From 1970 to 1973 Park was plagued by knee injuries that limited his play. In addition to crippling the defense, Park's absence was almost fatal to the Rangers power-play and penalty killing units.

Despite 25 goals, 57 assists, for 82 points in 1973-74, and his fifth All-Star berth in six years, he is still waiting for the Stanley Cup to come to New York. And, along with Walt Tkaczuk and Rod Gilbert, Brad Park will be a major factor in bringing the Cup home.

Brad Park topped the Rangers in scoring in 1973-74 with 25 goals and 57 assists for 82 points.

Brad Park attracts a crowd as he tries to
carry the puck against Atlanta.

derek sanderson

The Rangers have decided that it's high time for an overall face-lift. There'll be no more excuses.

After virtually giving ex-captain Vic Hadfield away, the Blueshirts did a 180-degree turnabout by trading for Derek Sanderson, the shaggy free-spirit whose hockey talent is rivaled only by his controversial quotes.

Sanderson, who spent most of the 1972-73-74 seasons shuttling between the WHA and NHL, signed a one-year contract with the Rangers in the Spring of 1974 for a reported $110,000.

That amounts to a pretty hefty gamble, and a gamble it is. Almost every prediction about Derek and the Rangers includes that biggest word in sports . . . IF!

Everyone knows that in the area of personal appearance, the Ranger are to ice-hockey what H. R. Haldeman was to the Administration. Mustaches were taboo, appearing in public without a jacket and tie was a no-no, and of course there was the ban on distracting extra-curricular activities available to any swinging bachelor in Gotham. Sanderson, of course, doesn't see that as a problem.

"I'm going to love New York," said Derek after learning of his new stomping grounds, "even though the fans hate me. This is Joe Namath's town. I'm only happy he's giving me a little piece of it."

Sanderson was one of many Bruins that Ranger fans loved to hate. In recent years, Rangers-Bruins games have taken on the characteristics of Roman arenas. Playoff series between the clubs were festivals of hate, with Sanderson the principal attraction. During the 1970 playoffs, Madison Square Garden was X-rated thanks to the more creative artistic efforts of the Rangers' fans. Bedsheet banners, boldly emblazoned, "DEREK IS AN (EXPLETIVE DELETED)" hung from the rafters. Even the Rangers got into the act, although to a slightly lesser extent.

"Derek Sanderson is a dirty player," proclaimed defenseman Brad Park in his book, *Play the Man.*

Derek Sanderson who joined the Rangers for the 1974-75 season is shown in action when he was a Bruin, playing against his future team.

Derek, naturally, countered with a few barbs of his own.

But all that's in the past now, and with Derek, one of the newest Rangers, even his worst enemies are willing to forgive and forget.

"All things said in the past are forgotten," said Brad Park.

The only thing that remains to be seen is, will Sanderson finally settle down and play hockey for the New Yorkers?

"Derek is no dummy," said Sanderson's ex-teammate, Phil Esposito. "He's a very intelligent man. He knows the score, I think he realizes its time to get serious about playing hockey. He knows this could be his last chance. If he blows it, he could be on the outside looking in.

"If Derek is in the right frame of mind," Espo continued, "he'll help the Rangers. If he wants to play, and I think he does, he'll definitely help them. He won't score 50 goals, but he could be good for 25 and can be a hell of a penalty killer."

As Ranger fans know all too well, fat salaries don't always provide the incentive. Sometimes they accomplish the opposite. The key, it would seem, lies in Derek's rapport with the conservative Emile Francis.

Francis seems optimistic. When asked about the Rangers' no facial hair rule with the wooly Sanderson looming in the future, the Cat replied, "I don't think that's very important."

But Derek can silence all his critics if he lives up to his brash statement on his future with the Rangers.

"I don't think they need more than Derek to win the Cup."

Derek Sanderson one of the more colorful players in the NHL, came to the Rangers from the Bruins in exchange for Walt McKechnie, after the 1973-74 season.

walt tkaczuk

Walter Tkaczuk has served the Rangers well as a great goal scorer and an effective penalty killer.

Walt Tkaczuk was known originally more for his tongue-twisting name than anything else. Yet the Rangers' center had two additional traits that soon became evident—size and strength.

His rookie year, 1968-69, with 12 goals and 36 points was unspectacular, but the Rangers knew, in time, Tkaczuk would develop the skill of a Jean Ratelle. Any doubts about his ability were erased as he went on to lead the Rangers in scoring for two straight years. Now everyone feels he has the talent to be named a superstar.

Walt epitomized Emile Francis' "strength down center" theory. His great power anchored the Rangers' "Bulldog Line" of 1969-70 which also boasted left wing Dave Balon and Billy Fairbairn.

Tkaczuk's durability was emphasized in the 1973-74 playoffs which he went through with a wired broken jaw. He joined Fairbairn to become one of the Rangers' top penalty killers. Tkaczuk's outstanding puck control and Fairbairn's tenacity thwarted many opposition power plays.

When Walt goes into the corners he most likely is the one to come out with the puck. His sense of balance and strength have given him the ability to crash into the boards, dig the disk out and then make a quick pass to a linemate. Tkaczuk's unselfishness sometimes accounts for one too many passes, but his prowess as a center showed when he almost "won" the Calder Trophy for Steve Vickers. Vickers' thirty goals can be traced to heads-up passes by Walt that Steve pushed into the net while standing at the edge of the crease.

Although he's too quiet to become the captain, there is no doubt that the unpronounceable name will one day take the Rangers on the road to the long awaited Stanley Cup.

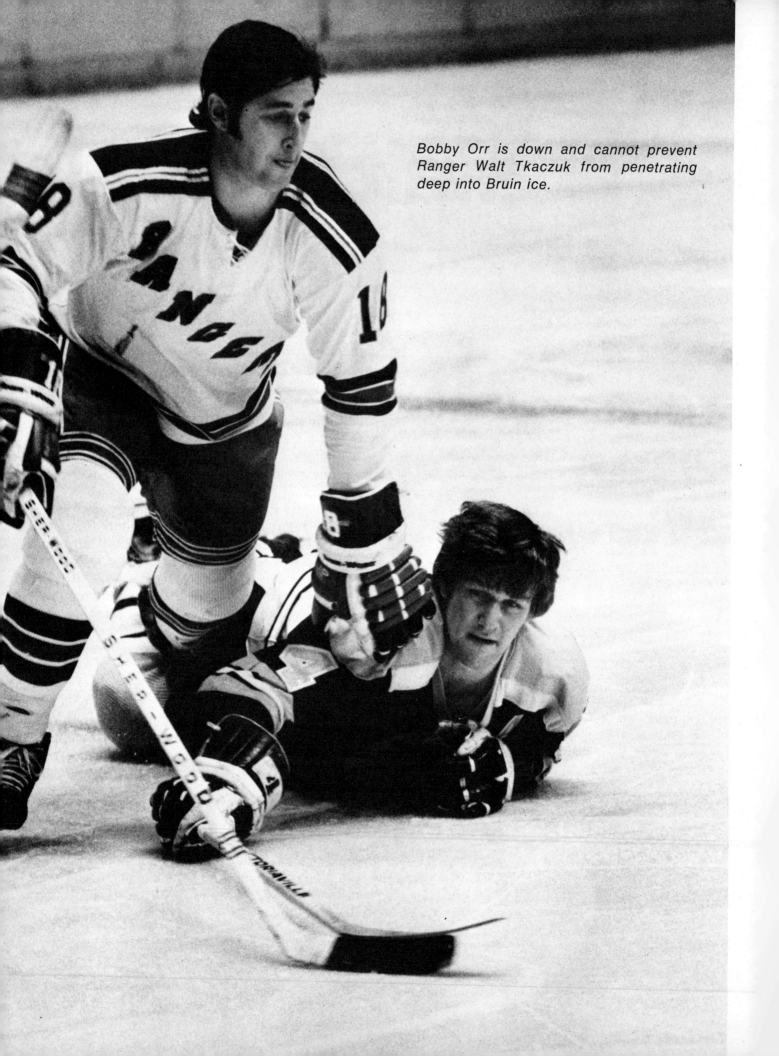

Bobby Orr is down and cannot prevent Ranger Walt Tkaczuk from penetrating deep into Bruin ice.

Walter Tkaczuk pursues puck carrier Phil Esposito up ice.

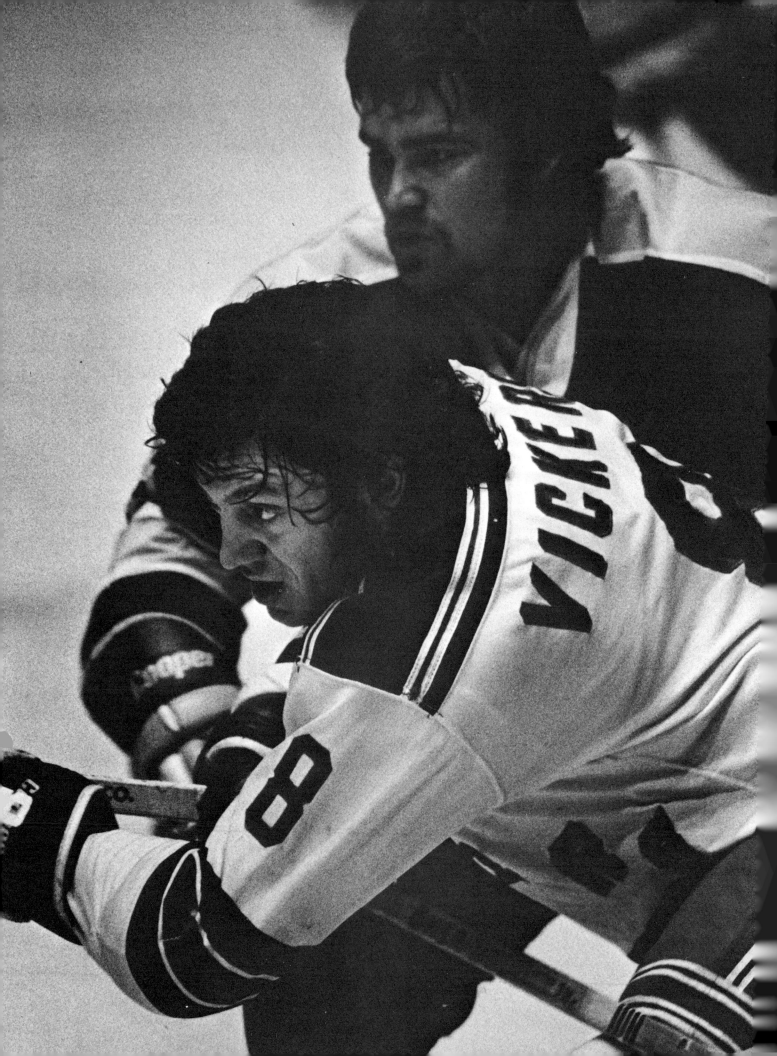

steve vickers

Steve Vickers was the NHL's Rookie of the Year in 1972-73. The Toronto native disproved the "sophomore jinx" when he scored 34 goals and tallied 24 assists for 58 points during the 1973-74 season.

In the 1973-74 season Steve Vickers bettered his 1973 Rookie of the Year statistics by four goals, finishing the regular schedule with 34 goals and 58 points. Seemingly, it was another solid scoring performance for the rugged left winger, bearing no inkling of the accursed malady known as "sophomore jinx"—to statistics watchers, that is.

Ah yes, but statistics, as they tell us, can be deceiving. And in Steve Vickers' case, the numbers would tell an infinitely clearer story if they were properly separated, and labeled: "Column A" for Pre-Larry Popein, and "Column B" for Post-Popein. The difference is staggering.

That, in a nutshell, was the saga of Steve Vickers' 1973-74 season. At times it seemed that there were two completely different men wearing sweater number eight for the Blueshirts. One was a listless, frustrated brooder; the other an enthusiastic, confident scoring machine.

Steve, like more than just a few of his teammates, found it a bit difficult adjusting to life under new coach Popein.

Midway through that season, the usually overpowering unit of Walt Tkaczuk, Bill Fairbairn and Vickers, was struggling through a scoring drought that made the Gobi Desert look like Hudson's Bay. Steve, himself, had not found the net in 17 straight games.

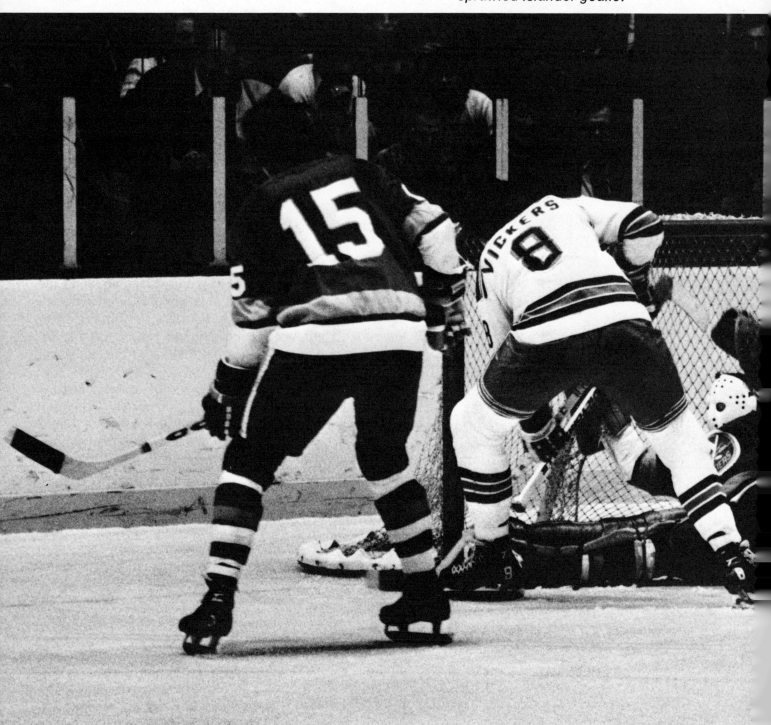

Steve Vickers is lifting the puck over a sprawled Islander goalie.

During the last week of December 1973 with the Rangers facing tough games against the raucous Philadelphia Flyers and the classy Montreal Canadiens, Vickers was benched by Popein. Something, the coach reasoned, had to be done to revitalize the line's scoring.

First it was newly-acquired Jack Egers getting a turn on the Bulldog Line's port side. Steve sat out most of that session against the Broad Street Bullies, and it didn't help Steve's case when the Rangers won the hard-fought game, 2–1. Understandably, he was disappointed and bitter.

Vickers remained a spectator for the next two games. This time it was the crowd-pleasing Bobby Rousseau who manned Steve's regular left wing slot. The artistic Rousseau scored in a 4–3 Rangers' win over the North Stars—good for the Rangers, bad for Vickers. The brooding sophomore was rapidly losing his self-confidence.

Linemates Tkaczuk and Fairbairn were quick to defend their mate. "If the coach is going to change our line," said an indignant Fairbairn, "he may as well bench all of us because we're all not scoring. It's not any one man's fault."

Tkaczuk was a bit more diplomatic. "What's wrong with our line?" mused the soft-spoken center. "The only thing is the puck won't go in for us."

On January 10th, 1974 the slumping New Yorkers crawled away from Buffalo after a 7–2 butchering at the hands of the Sabres. Five hours after the final buzzer, Larry Popein was no longer the Ranger coach.

General manager Emile Francis reassumed the Blueshirts coaching chores for the third time in nine years.

As if by magic, the Rangers, and Vickers in particular, did a complete turnabout. Under the new-old Francis regime the Rangers lost only two of their next 18 games with Steve reversing his nose dive and netting an amazing 16 goals. The night after Popein's sudden departure, Steve ended his 17-game goal drought by scoring one in a 6–1 Ranger romp over the Vancouver Canucks. It was Vickers again in the very next Ranger outing, as he potted the winner against the California Golden Seals.

*Steve Vickers and the Sabres' Jim Schoen-
feld eye the action.*

Joyous signs of Vickers' rejuvenation continued. He scored his third career hat trick against the Rangers' suburban neighbors, the New York Islanders.

As soon as Francis had resumed as coach, he huddled with Vickers to iron out the youngster's troubles. Francis was firm, but understanding. Steve emerged from their private meeting looking, and feeling, like a new man.

"He did it in a polite, positive way," said Vickers, recounting his rap session with the Cat. "And it certainly helped."

Helped isn't the word. Francis' wondrous exorcism transformed an uncertain starter with anemic scoring statistics into the club's second leading goal-getter. Steve finished the season strong and continued his heroics into the playoffs.

His future is bright.

*Steve Vickers checks a Montreal Cana-
dien.*